PROUDLY
RED and BLACK
• • •
Stories of African
and Native Americans

To
Chief Osceola Townsend,
Alice Walker,
Rene Sibanacan,
Hector Rodriguez,
and other keepers
of this dual flame

Books by **William Loren Katz**

Black Indians

The Lincoln Brigade
(with Marc Crawford)

Breaking the Chains

P·R·O·U·D·L·Y
RED and BLACK
·   ·   ·
Stories of African
and Native Americans

William Loren Katz
and
Paula A. Franklin

Atheneum   1993   New York

Maxwell Macmillan Canada
Toronto

Maxwell Macmillan International
New York   Oxford   Singapore   Sydney

Atheneum
Macmillan Publishing Company
866 Third Avenue
New York, NY 10022

Maxwell Macmillan Canada, Inc.
1200 Eglinton Avenue East
Suite 200
Don Mills, Ontario M3C 3N1

Macmillan Publishing Company is part of the Maxwell Communication Group of Companies.

First edition

Printed in the United States of America

10 9 8 7 6 5 4 3 2 1

Book design by Eileen Burke

The text of this book is set in Palatino.

Library of Congress Cataloging-in-Publication Data

Katz, William Loren.
    Proudly Red and Black: stories of African and Native Americans / by William Loren Katz and Paula Angle Franklin.—1st ed.
        p.   cm.
    Includes bibliographical references (p. 83) and index.
    Summary: Brief biographies of people of mixed Native American and African ancestry, who, despite barriers, made their mark on history, including trader Paul Cuffe, frontiersman Edward Rose, Seminole leader John Horse, and sculptress Edmonia Lewis.
    ISBN 0-689-31801-4
    1. Racially mixed people—United States—Biography—Juvenile literature. 2. Afro-Americans—Biography—Juvenile literature. 3. Indians of North America—Biography—Juvenile literature. 4. Afro-Americans—Relations with Indians—Juvenile literature. [1. Racially mixed people—Biography. 2. Afro-Americans—Biography. 3. Indians of North America—Biography. 4. Afro-Americans—Relations with Indians.] I. Franklin, Paula Angle, 1928–   . II. Title.
E184.A1K32   1993
970.004′043—dc20
    [B]   92–36119

CONTENTS

Rap singer LL Cool J proudly holds up a book about some of his ancestors who were both Native American and African.

INTRODUCTION

The people whose life stories you will read about in this book have something in common. Each one is a unique American mixture that includes both African-American and Native American racial groups. Millions of other Americans also share this "only in America" mixture.

Blacks and Indians have a special relationship. It developed mainly because of white Europeans, who began settling in America in the 1500s. They enslaved many Native Americans, who had been living here for centuries. And they also brought people from Africa as slaves. Blacks and Indians soon found that, as people of color, they faced similar problems.

Native American slaves escaped to the forests they knew. Many then returned for their African friends. Blacks and Indians often helped one another by forming colonies in the woods or mountains, far from white settlements. Men and women from the two racial groups fell in love, married, and had children. Thus the two peoples developed friendships, alliances, and a blending of families.

Most Americans, including blacks and Indians, do not know much about the relationship between these two peoples. During the early years of American history, many communities lacked written records. And even after slavery came to an end, discrimination against people of color limited their opportunities to record their history and preserve it for later generations. So, for many people who have this rich background, it is a hidden heritage.

This book describes the lives of people who were of mixed Native American and African ancestry. Each was able to make a mark on the world. All of them faced barriers, but they never gave up in their efforts to succeed in the United States of America.

William Loren Katz
Paula A. Franklin

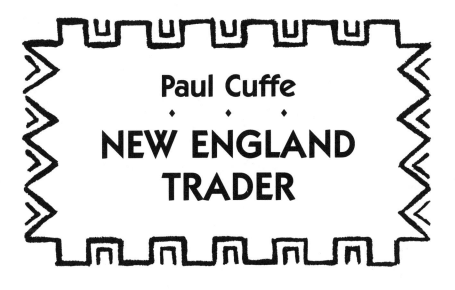

Paul Cuffe
◆　◆　◆
NEW ENGLAND TRADER

The streets were hardly more than dusty paths. Here and there stood rickety wooden houses, separated by vacant lots. The few big buildings seemed out of place. One was the White House, where the president lived. Another—just an empty shell—was the Capitol, where Congress would eventually meet.

This was Washington, D.C., in 1812. The city had been founded only a few years earlier. Still, though it didn't look like much yet, it was the headquarters of the United States government. And New Englander Paul Cuffe was happy to be there. He was on his way to see the president, James Madison.

Cuffe had come a long way. At that time a trip from Massachusetts to Washington took several days. But the journey had been a long one in other ways, too. Cuffe, born to an African father and a Native American mother, had started life as a poor sailor. Now he was the richest man of color in the United States.

♦   ♦   ♦

Paul Cuffe's parents came from two very different worlds. His father, known as Cuffe Slocum, was born in Africa. His mother, Ruth Moses, was a Wampanoag Indian from the Massachusetts island of Martha's Vineyard.

Paul Cuffe's father may have come from Ghana. His first name was probably Kofi, a common name there. In any case, he was brought to America as a slave in the 1720s. When he arrived he was bought by Ebenezer Slocum, who lived in the coastal town of Dartmouth, Massachusetts. At this time there were slaves in all the American colonies. New England, however, did not have many compared to the South. Cuffe probably worked in the Slocum house as a servant. He may have done odd jobs to earn money. This might have been how he was able to buy his freedom by 1746. In that year he and Ruth Moses were married.

Ruth Moses was born into the Indian nation of the Wampanoag, who lived in eastern Massachusetts. They were the first people the Pilgrims met when they arrived from England to settle at Plymouth in 1620. One of the first things the Pilgrims did was to sign a treaty of friendship with a Wampanoag leader named Massasoit. Unfortunately, good feeling between whites and Native Americans didn't last very long. The main problem was that whites took Indian land, and the Indians fought to keep it. In the 1670s a son of Massasoit, Metacomet, led an all-out war of New England Indians against the whites. After many battles, the Indians lost. Some of them were seized as slaves. Others moved away. By the time Ruth

In the only known picture of him, Paul Cuffe is shown in silhouette with his ship, *Traveller,* in 1812.

Moses was born, there were only a few hundred Wampanoag Indians in Massachusetts. Most of them lived on small reservations.

◆　　　◆　　　◆

When Cuffe Slocum and Ruth Moses were first married, they lived among her people. Later they bought land on the Massachusetts mainland. Eventually they had ten children. Paul, the seventh, was born in 1759. The family made a living by farming and fishing.

Young Paul had little time for school, although he did learn to read and write. His father died when he was only thirteen. This meant that he and his brothers and sisters had to take on extra responsibilities at an early age.

Living within sight and sound of the ocean, Paul wanted to go to sea. He first became a "marineer," as he put it, when he was sixteen. Paul made many voyages on the sailing ships of the day. Sometimes they hunted whales. (Whale oil was prized as fuel for lamps.) Sometimes they carried cargo back and forth to other colonies or to the West Indies.

Paul could see that the traders who owned ships made more money than sailors did. So he and his older brother David built their own ship and went into business for themselves. Paul soon earned enough to begin investing in other ships, too. This meant that he would help pay for expenses—cargo, sailors' wages, and so on—and earn a share of the profits.

By the time Paul was in his early twenties, he was making a good living. It was time to get married. Interestingly, he turned to the Wampanoag Indian nation, just as his father had for his bride. Her name was Alice Pequit, and the wedding took place in 1783. On the marriage certificate Paul's last name appeared as "Cuffe." Most of the family had now taken their father's first name as their last. They may have done so out of pride in Africa.

♦   ♦   ♦

By the time Paul and Alice Cuffe were married, in 1783, the American colonists had declared their independence from England. (One of the first Americans to die in the cause of independence, Crispus Attucks, was apparently of mixed African and Natick Indian parentage.) Americans had fought and won a revolution. And they had formed a new nation, the United States of America.

The Declaration of Independence proclaimed that "all men are created equal." In the new United States, many states, especially those in New England, were doing away with slavery. But real equality did not exist for either African Americans or Native Americans. Black people were still enslaved in many parts of the United States. Even free African Americans were not truly free. In most states they could not vote or testify in court against a white person. Many schools and occupations were closed to them. As for Indians, some were slaves, others were free but not U.S. citizens. When the whites wanted Indian land, they took it—peacefully if possible, by force if necessary. Most white people believed that both blacks and Indians were inferior human beings.

♦   ♦   ♦

Simply by prospering, Paul Cuffe proved that he was as capable as anyone else. In less than twenty years he was worth ten thousand dollars—a lot of money in those times.

Cuffe and the sailors he hired—most of them African Americans—always behaved modestly and quietly. This made sense, because whites were hard on blacks they regarded as "uppity." At the same time, though, Cuffe was a determined man. When he faced a problem, he tried to do something about it.

Take the matter of taxes and voting. Cuffe and other men of color in Massachusetts had to pay taxes on their property. But they were not allowed to vote. This was certainly a case of taxation without representation—one of the chief complaints of the colonists against England. In 1779 Paul Cuffe, his brother John, and others protested by refusing to pay their taxes. After being arrested and jailed, they paid up. But they continued to protest. In 1783 Massachusetts granted its black citizens the right to vote. "For this triumph of justice," wrote a black New Yorker, everyone owed "a tribute of respect to John and Paul Cuffe."

Another problem had to do with education for the Cuffes' sons and daughters. (Paul and Alice had seven children.) The town of Westport, where the family lived, had no school. Cuffe suggested that the townspeople raise money and build one. The response was poor. Whites probably did not want their children going to school with children of color. So Cuffe simply built the school himself on his own land. All the children of the town were welcome, and all attended.

In his struggles Cuffe had support from some of the whites of Westport. Most of them were merchants like him. And most of them were Quakers—members of the religious group known officially as the Society of Friends. Cuffe attended their Sunday meetings. He liked the Quakers' simplicity and their interest in good causes. For instance, most Quakers strongly opposed slavery. Some even helped slaves escape. The Quaker faith meant a great deal to Cuffe. He became an official member in 1808, when he was forty-nine.

In this Rhode Island school African-American and Native American children were given instruction together in the early nineteenth century.

* * *

When he was young, Cuffe had apparently thought of himself as both African and Indian. By the early 1800s, however, he identified more strongly with his African heritage. At that time he became interested in a cause that would absorb him for the rest of his life. This was African colonization—settling former slaves in colonies in Africa.

Many people who opposed slavery believed in African colonization. They thought that it was the best way to encourage slave owners to free their slaves. The first colony for ex-slaves was started by the English in Sierra Leone. Its colonists were black people who had escaped to England or from slave ships.

At first Cuffe was interested in African colonization only for the sake of Africans. He wanted to convert them to Christianity. He also thought that trained African Americans could teach Africans useful skills. Later Cuffe wanted colonization for the sake of African Americans as well. He thought it offered them their only chance for a safe and happy future.

Cuffe made two trips to Sierra Leone. The first time, in 1811, he traded goods and looked over the colony. He also visited England and learned more about colonization efforts. But he ran into trouble when he got back to the United States. While he was away Congress had passed a law forbidding trade with England. Without meaning to, Cuffe had broken the law by bringing in goods from an English colony, Sierra Leone. The government seized his goods. This was why Cuffe went to see President Madison in 1812. He arranged to have his goods returned. He also had a chance to urge that the government help sponsor African colonization.

Cuffe wanted to go back to Africa as soon as he could. But he had to wait several years until a war with England (the War of 1812) was over. Then he took with him thirty-eight settlers, who landed early in 1816. This action did a lot to make Americans aware of African colonization. That same year people organized a group that eventually sponsored another African colony, Liberia. In the long run, though, African colonization did not win much support in the United States. Sending former slaves to Africa cost a lot of money. More important, most ex-slaves simply did not want to leave the United States.

Paul Cuffe lived only about a year after he returned from his second trip to Sierra Leone. A newspaper reporting his death in September 1817 spoke of him as "much esteemed by all classes of people for his morality, truth, and intelligence." Nothing better illustrates these qualities, or the times in which he lived, than a brief incident Cuffe described in his own journal. On his way home from seeing the president in 1812, he stopped at an inn in Baltimore.

> When I arrived in Baltimore they utterly refused to take me in the tavern, or to get me a dinner, unless I would go back among the servants. This I refused. Not as I thought myself better than the servants, but from the nature of the case.

Paul Cuffe was a modest man. But he was a proud man, too.

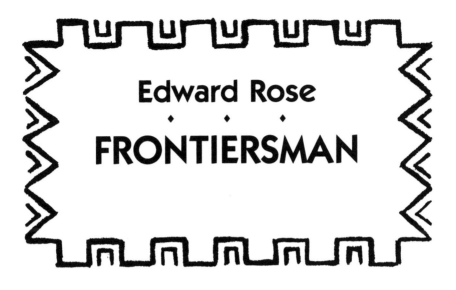

Edward Rose
• • •
FRONTIERSMAN

"The Americans are great travellers," wrote a visiting Englishman when our country was young. "They are also a migrating people," he went on. Even when they were doing well, he noted, they would move if they thought they could do better somewhere else.

When white Americans moved, they usually moved west. Beyond the frontier of settled farms and towns, land was cheap. It was not empty, because Native Americans lived there. But the push of new settlers drove the Indians aside. The Indians were forced to keep moving even farther west.

In colonial times the West lay in the foothills of the Appalachian Mountains. Then came independence. The population grew, and more and more Americans wanted land of their own. Covered wagons creaked over the mountains. Pioneers cleared new farms on the prairies beyond. The West was now the valleys of the many rivers that flowed westward into the great Mississippi.

Then, almost overnight, the United States just about doubled its size. This happened in 1803, when the nation bought a huge piece of land, the Louisiana Purchase, from France. Much bigger than the present-day state of Louisiana, this new West extended all the way from the Mississippi River to the Rocky Mountains.

Hardly anyone knew what the Louisiana Purchase was like. So President Thomas Jefferson sent out two men, Meriwether Lewis and William Clark, to explore and report. Their expedition included Sacagawea, a Shoshone Indian woman who served as guide and interpreter. Another member was Clark's black servant, York. Clark (whose grammar and spelling were a bit shaky) wrote about one encounter: "Those Indians wer much astonished at my Servent, they never Saw a black man before, all flocked around him & examin him from top to toe."

The West explored by Lewis and Clark was a land of grassy, treeless plains and steep mountains. It was a land of beavers and otters and buffalo. And it was the home of the proud Plains Indians, who pitched their tepees wherever game animals were plentiful.

◆   ◆   ◆

Into this West came Edward Rose. He is much more of a mystery man than Paul Cuffe. No one quotes him directly, and there are no known writings of his. (It's quite possible that he couldn't read or write. In those days few people could.) Unlike Cuffe, he lived in a world where written records and accounts were scarce. It was also a world that valued tall tales and dramatic exploits. So some of the exciting stories told about Rose may never have happened, or may have happened to someone else.

No one knows when Edward Rose was born, but it may have been in the 1780s. No one knows where he was born, either, though some said Louisville, Kentucky. His father was a white trader; his mother was part Cherokee and part African American. According to one story Rose was an escaped slave. According to another tale he was for a time a pirate on the Mississippi River. Perhaps he was both.

We do know that Rose made his first appearance on the stage of history at St. Louis, in 1807. At that time he joined an expedition led by a man named Manuel Lisa. Lisa, of Hispanic descent, planned to row up the Missouri River and build trading posts. He wanted furs.

◆　　　◆　　　◆

Beavers are interesting as the engineers of the animal world. They have teeth so sharp and powerful that they can cut down trees. They eat twigs and use tree branches to build dams. Beaver dams protect the underwater lodges in which colonies of beavers live. Beavers also played a special role in American history because of their glossy brown fur.

About 1600, men in Europe started wearing felt hats made of beaver fur. Beaver in Europe soon became scarce. But North America offered vast new supplies. All the early colonists—English, Dutch, and French—traded with Native American hunters for beaver pelts. Naturally, the beaver supply dwindled as settlements ate up the forests in which beavers lived. So people were constantly looking for new sources beyond the frontier. It is said that the beaver was the greatest single cause of exploration in North America.

Beaver was certainly one of the things Lewis and Clark were looking for when they traveled through the Louisiana Purchase. They found ample supplies and reported their finds. Manuel Lisa was one of the first people to organize an expedition to take advantage of their discoveries.

•　　•　　•

When Edward Rose joined Lisa's band he was a strong young man with a scarred forehead and a disfigured nose—slashed, some said, in a fight. (The Indians called him Cut Nose.) Those who knew him always mentioned his grim and moody ways. Washington Irving, who wrote two books about the fur trade, calls him "dogged, sullen, silent." Rose also had a reputation for lawlessness. But this may have been due to his fierce appearance. In the words of one historian, "everything definite that is known of him is entirely to his credit." If we judge Rose only on the record, this expert continues, "he would stand as high as any character in the history of the fur trade."

Rose was one of Lisa's company of forty-two, including some men who had traveled with Lewis and Clark. The expedition left St. Louis in April 1807. As they rowed their heavy keelboat north in the summer heat, they passed several Native American villages. Sometimes the Indians were friendly, sometimes not. But there were no serious problems. By fall the men had arrived in what is now Montana. They rowed up the Yellowstone River to the Bighorn, where they built a trading post, Fort Manuel. It was the first European trading post in this region.

Rose and the other men in Lisa's expedition spent the cold, snowy winter trading with the local Indians for bea-

Black fur trappers, like Edward Rose, helped explore the frontier.

ver and other pelts. When the river ice broke and the weather warmed up in the spring, the men loaded the furs onto their keelboat and set off down the river for St. Louis. One man—Rose—remained behind.

♦   ♦   ♦

Edward Rose had gone to live with a Native American nation we call the Crows. (Their name for themselves was Absarokas, which means "sparrow hawks" or "crows" in their own language.) Like other Plains peoples, the Crows lived by hunting buffalo. They not only ate buffalo meat and wore clothing of buffalo hide and fur, they also lived in tepees made from buffalo skin, fought using buffalo-hide shields, and even burned buffalo droppings as fuel.

Native Americans welcomed non-Indians who chose to live among them. (They were much more hospitable than whites were to nonwhites.) Some of these "adopted" Indians were people captured in warfare. More often, as in the case of Edward Rose, the non-Indians were fur traders. Many of them married Indian women.

No one knows whether Edward Rose had a Native American wife. He probably did, because he lived with various Indian bands off and on for at least the next fifteen years. It is known that he learned Crow customs and the Crow language, and was respected as a leader. He learned other Indian languages, too, as well as the sign language that different Plains peoples used to communicate with one another. Certainly Rose became an important figure on the frontier, for he knew the land and the ways of both Indians and Europeans.

Rose's black heritage gave him a special advantage. African Americans, less prejudiced toward Indians, got along with them better than whites did. One expert on the West, Colonel James Stevenson, claimed that "the old fur traders always got a Negro if possible to negotiate for

Another trapper, Jim Pierce, also served as cook and guide
for expeditions into the wilderness.

them with the Indians" because "they could manage them
better than white men, with less friction." Indians had no
racial prejudices and so were more than willing to accept
African Americans as equals.

◆　　◆　　◆

It was spring in the year 1811. Along the upper Missouri
River the air was sweet with the smell of wildflowers. An
expedition of sixty people, most of them white fur traders,
was camping near a village of Arikara Indians in what is
now South Dakota. Led by Wilson Price Hunt, the group

was bound for Astoria, a trading post on the coast of present-day Oregon.

Hunt had planned to row up the Missouri as far as he could, traveling through the land of the Sioux and Blackfeet. But trappers he met on the way had told him that this route was dangerous. They advised him to leave the Missouri at the Arikara village and go west on land, through Crow territory. Hunt decided to follow their advice. He traded his boats for horses. But his guides didn't know the way.

Now Edward Rose entered the picture. He may have been traveling with the men for some time, but Hunt's journal first mentions him on June 13. Yes, he agreed, he would guide the expedition across the land he knew so well.

The group set out in mid-July. Rose was a good guide. He was especially helpful when the traders met up with Crows. They knew and respected him, and he knew their language. One night, however, someone told Hunt that Rose was plotting trouble. He was going to talk several of the men into deserting, taking with them their horses and supplies. Hunt believed this story, though there was never any evidence for it. In his journal he referred to Rose as "a very bad fellow full of daring."

By early September the expedition had crossed Crow country into the foothills of the Rockies. Hunt dismissed Rose and paid him off. Rose was happy to remain with his friends the Crows. After that, the Astorians, as Hunt's group was called, got into a lot of trouble on their westward journey. They lost their way, they lost their horses, and some of them lost their lives. Only forty-two members of the original expedition finally reached Astoria early in 1812.

◆   ◆   ◆

Several years passed. Rose seemed to have dropped out of sight. Apparently he lived with the Crows and, later, with the Arikaras. Then, in the spring of 1823, he appeared again near the same Arikara village on the upper Missouri River. And again he came to the aid of a fur-trading expedition. This one was led by an ambitious man named William Ashley.

Ashley was trying a new idea. Why should fur traders rely on Native American middlemen to supply pelts? Why shouldn't they send their own trappers into the Rockies? A year earlier he had advertised for "enterprising young men" to work for him as hunters. Those who signed on as "mountain men" included Jedediah Smith, Jim Bridger, and Mike Fink.

Ashley's 1822 expedition had not been a success, but now he was trying a second time. Smith and Bridger had signed on again. Other noted mountain men in the group included James Clyman and Hugh Glass. Now Ashley also had the services of Edward Rose as guide and interpreter. He joined the expedition late in May, as it was preparing to leave the Missouri and strike out overland.

This time the problem was not so much unfamiliar terrain as Indian hostility. The Arikaras had been important suppliers in the fur trade. Now it looked as if they were being shoved aside by non-Indian mountain men. At the village, Rose sensed trouble. But Ashley refused to listen to his warnings.

Suddenly, early on a June morning, the Indians attacked. Some of Ashley's men took shelter on the keelboats in the river. But several others, including Rose, Glass, and

Clyman, were pinned down by heavy arrow and rifle fire on an exposed sandbar. They eventually escaped by throwing down their guns and swimming to the boats. Fourteen trappers were killed. Clyman wrote afterward:

> Before meeting with this defeat, I think few men had stronger ideas of their bravery and disregard of fear than I had but standing on a bear [bare] and open sand barr [bar] to be shot at from behind a picketed Indian village was more than I had contracted for and somewhat cooled my courage.

Ashley wanted revenge, so he sent for help. The army supplied over two hundred men, commanded by Colonel Henry Leavenworth. By August a mixed force of trappers, soldiers, and their Sioux allies had gathered at the Arikara village. After a two-day pitched battle, the Arikaras surrendered. Because Leavenworth feared a trap, he sent Edward Rose alone to discuss peace terms with the Arikaras. Only after he returned safely did everyone breathe easy. No wonder Leavenworth praised Rose as a "brave and enterprising man."

Rose spent the next two years with Smith, Clyman, and other mountain men, exploring the Rocky Mountains. During this time they probably became the first non-Indians to discover the South Pass through the Rockies. It turned out to be the only practical wagon route across the northern mountains, and later became part of the Oregon Trail. One writer described the band as "the most significant group of continental explorers ever brought together."

Rose's last definite appearance was in 1825, when he

joined another expedition as an interpreter. This time he served an army force led by General Henry Atkinson and Major Benjamin O'Fallon. Their aim was to impress Native Americans with the friendship—and power—of the United States. Rowing up the Missouri in the early summer, they stopped often to meet various bands of Plains Indians. Gifts were exchanged and treaties signed. Army reports mention Rose's useful service as an interpreter. He also won praise as a buffalo hunter. One report tells how he brought down six of the animals in about as many minutes.

◆　　◆　　◆

After his work in the 1820s Rose probably returned to live with the Crows. Various tales were told about his adventures. Some of these may have actually involved Jim Beckwourth, a black frontiersman who also lived among the Crows. (On the other hand, some of the exploits Beckwourth tells about himself may have really happened to Rose.)

No one knows for certain when or how Edward Rose met his death. It probably happened somewhere on the northern Great Plains, where he had lived for so long. Old maps of the upper Missouri valley show a "Cut Nose Butte" near the mouth of the Yellowstone River. And farther to the west, at the mouth of the Milk River, these same maps show a cross marked "Rose's Grave."

Although much is unknown about Edward Rose, there seems no reason to doubt the opinion of Reuben Holmes. This army officer, a member of the Atkinson-O'Fallon expedition, wrote an account of the frontiersman that included this judgment:

He was as cunning as a prairie wolf. He was a perfect woodsman. He could endure any kind of fatigue and privation as well as the best trained Indians. He studied men. There was nothing that an Indian could do, that Rose did not make himself master of. He knew all that Indians knew. He was a great man in his situation.

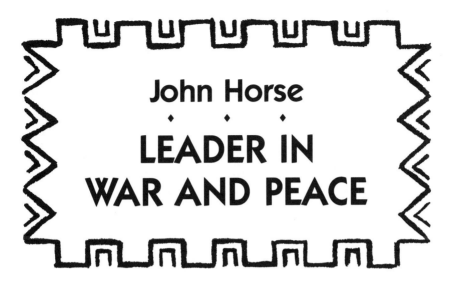

John Horse
♦ ♦ ♦
LEADER IN
WAR AND PEACE

He was a man of many names. One was Cowaya (some-times spelled Ca-Wy-Ya). Another was John Horse. This name also took the form of Juan Caballo, the same words in Spanish. To many he was known by a nickname, Go-pher John. It came from a practical joke the teenage boy played on an army officer. Young John sold the man several turtles of a kind called "gopher" terrapins. Then he some-how got hold of the same terrapins and sold them to the officer again. Even the officer apparently enjoyed the boy's prank.

When John Horse grew up, he became an unusual leader. He was a man respected by both Native and Af-rican Americans, and by whites as well. His story begins in Florida.

♦ ♦ ♦

Native Americans once made their homes throughout the southeastern United States. Place names like Chattahoochee, Okefenokee, Tallahassee, Chattanooga, and Tuscaloosa are all living reminders of their presence. The best known of these Indians were the Creeks, Cherokees, Chickasaws, and Choctaws. Clustered in big villages, they lived by farming and hunting.

Europeans began settling in this southeastern region in the 1500s. There were the English along the Atlantic coast, the Spanish in Florida, and the French along the Mississippi River. Native Americans, strong and numerous, did well by playing these three groups against each other. Indians exchanged deerskins, furs, and the services of their fighting men for livestock, guns, and other trade goods. Usually they could get a better deal from one group of Europeans by threatening to take their trade to another. The Creeks, who were very good at this sort of bargaining, became especially powerful.

In all the wheeling and dealing of the colonial period, Florida was a special place. Until 1819 it wasn't part of the United States, but was claimed by Spain or England. Neither country could control this faraway colony, so its woods and swamps attracted a lot of people from the North American colonies. They fell into two main groups: former slaves and members of the Creek nation.

Thousands of Africans were held in slavery in the southern colonies. Few were ever allowed to earn their freedom. The only way they could gain it was by escaping. If they were caught they faced terrible punishments, including death. But if they reached Florida, most were safe from capture. Former slaves who had escaped to live in their own communities were called Maroons, from the Spanish word *cimarrón*, meaning "wild" or "runaway."

John Horse, the leader of the black Seminoles for more than thirty years

The other group that settled in Florida was made up of Creeks who had left the settlements of their nation in Alabama and Georgia. Many wanted to escape Indian-white power struggles and lead the simpler life of earlier times. These Creeks who left for Florida were called Seminoles. The word meant "runaways" in the Creek language.

In Florida, black Maroons and Seminoles became allies. In some places they married and settled together. In other places they formed separate communities that existed side by side. Whites believed the Africans were slaves of the Indians, but they lived in almost complete freedom. All they had to do was give their Seminole "owners" a share of the crops they produced. According to a white U.S. officer, "The Negroes of the Seminole Indians . . . are slaves but in name." This group, too, gained a new name, black Seminoles.

Black Seminoles had two big advantages in Florida. They knew much more about agriculture than the Seminoles did. They had been farmers in Africa and worked mostly as farmers in the American colonies. (They may well have taught the Seminoles how to grow rice.) Also, black people spoke English, which most Seminoles did not. This skill made them useful as interpreters.

◆　　◆　　◆

Interpreting was one of John Horse's many skills. This black Seminole was born around 1812 in northern Florida. His father was a Seminole, his mother an African American. Nothing is known of his childhood. He never learned to read or write. But he did learn both the Creek language of his father and the English of his mother. In later life he spoke both languages well enough to be a master diplomat.

Horse grew up in a troubled time. Americans from the East were moving across the Appalachian Mountains and taking Indian land. Some Native Americans fled farther west. Others, like the Creeks, fought back. Army troops defeated them at Horseshoe Bend, Alabama, in 1814. Then U.S. forces invaded Florida to burn black and Seminole villages and capture Spanish towns. U.S. slaveholders were furious that their slaves could escape to Florida and live there. They had demanded the government recapture their slaves and return them. The main result of this First Seminole War (1816–1818) was to force Spain to sell Florida to the United States.

Now all the southeastern Indian nations were under U.S. control. By treaty, they gave up much of their land and accepted reservations. Even there they prospered as farmers. (Many, especially among the Creeks, owned plantations worked by slaves.) They invited Christian missionaries to set up churches and schools. They developed law codes. An outstanding Cherokee, Sequoya, invented an alphabet so that his language could be written down for the first time. Because of all this acceptance of white ways, the major southeastern Indian nations—Creeks, Cherokees, Chickasaws, Chocktaws, and Seminoles— were to become known as the "Five Civilized Tribes." European Americans contrasted them with the "wild" peoples of the plains, such as the Crows.

◆　　　◆　　　◆

Clearly, most Native Americans of the Southeast had learned to be what white Americans regarded as model citizens. But they still had good land, and the whites wanted it. In 1830 Congress passed an important law, the Indian Removal Act. It allowed the president to place Indians on territories west of the Mississippi River in exchange for their land in the East. The government encouraged Native Americans to move west. But there was a catch: If the Indians wouldn't move willingly, the government would use force.

This is just what happened during the next few years. First the Choctaws, then the Creeks, and then the Chickasaws had to give up almost everything they owned. Many had to walk to their new homes in Indian Territory (what is now Oklahoma). When the Cherokees were moved, so many died on the way that their route is still called the "Trail of Tears."

Most of the Seminoles refused to go. Their situation was special. Whites not only wanted Indian land in Florida, they also wanted to reclaim the black Seminoles as slaves. The Seminoles agreed that they would never allow this to happen. The result was the Second Seminole War, which began in 1835.

The best known of the Seminole leaders was Osceola, a smart military commander and spellbinding speaker. One of his chief advisers was John Horse, now a young man in his twenties. Whites described him as tall, slim, and "ginger-colored," with long, wavy hair. He was noted for his proud posture, his tact as a diplomat, and his skill as a rifleman.

Osceola, Horse, and other fighters hid women and children in the swamps. They were then free to carry on guerrilla warfare against army troops. U.S. officers agreed that the Seminoles "fought as long as they had life through the influence of the leading Negroes." According to U.S. General Sidney Jesup, it was "a Negro, not an Indian, war."

The two sides agreed to a cease-fire in 1837. (Horse's name appeared on the document as John Ca-Wy-Ya.) The Seminoles agreed to move west. And the government agreed that the black Seminoles could go, too. But in just a few weeks the government went back on its word by enslaving black Seminoles who had surrendered. So the war started up again. Osceola, Horse, and another leader named Wild Cat led a daring raid to free several black Seminoles. Later that year, however, these three leaders and others were treacherously captured while under a flag of truce.

Osceola died in prison. But Horse, Wild Cat, and others fasted until they could slip through the prison bars and escape. "We resolved to make our escape or die in the attempt," Wild Cat later wrote. The war resumed, with each side claiming victories. In the end, however, the African and other Seminoles could not win out against the larger forces opposing them. Most of them gave up early in 1838 and agreed to move to Indian Territory. The army promised that African Seminoles would remain free and "should be sent to the west, as a part of the Seminole nation."

John Horse, the last leader to surrender, gave up in April. After traveling to Indian Territory, he returned to Florida. There, serving as a guide and interpreter, he helped persuade additional red and black Seminoles to give themselves up. Almost everyone did so. About three hundred, however, remained in the Everglades. Their descendants still live there, and still claim Florida as theirs.

The Second Seminole War officially ended in 1842. It had cost the United States an untold number of Seminole dead, 1,500 U.S. soldiers killed, and forty million U.S. dollars spent.

> We will go with the Indians to our new home. . . . We do not live for ourselves only, but for our wives & children who are as dear to us as those of any other men. When we reach our home we hope we shall be permitted to remain while the woods remain green, and the water runs. . . . All the black people are contented I hope.

So wrote a black Seminole named Abraham to the U.S. general in charge of the Florida campaign. Abraham, Horse, and others like them hoped for the best from their new life in Indian Territory. But they were actually worse off than before.

The main problem was that the Seminoles and their black allies were located in the midst of Creek territory. Many Creeks claimed that the black Seminoles included former slaves of theirs who had escaped earlier. When blacks refused to give themselves up, the Creeks hunted them down and seized them by force. Even when the Creeks did not claim black Seminoles as their own property, they wanted to treat them as slaves.

In 1844 Wild Cat, with Horse as interpreter, headed a delegation to Washington, D.C. Its members asked the government to protect all Seminoles from the Creeks. The authorities refused. In fact, a few years later the government went a step further and declared that the army had had no right to guarantee the freedom of the black Seminoles.

Two young black Seminole women photographed in the early twentieth century in Florida

Horse must have despaired. In 1849 he led a group of his people to a location in what is now central Oklahoma. There he founded Wewoka as a "city of refuge." Armed cavalrymen patrolled its outskirts to guard against slave raiders. But nearby Creeks demanded that the blacks give up their guns.

For Horse, there now seemed to be only one solution. That was to leave Indian Territory and the United States altogether. In 1850 he led several hundred black Seminoles south into Mexico, a country that had abolished slavery twenty years earlier. At the same time, Wild Cat guided a group of Seminoles southward across the Rio Grande into Mexico.

The newcomers got permission from the Mexican government to settle in northern Mexico. Along with land they received tools, plows, and animals for farming. In exchange, they agreed to act as a sort of border defense corps. They were experienced fighters. The Mexicans hoped that they would protect Mexican territory from Texas slave raiders and from Commanches, Kiowas, and Apaches.

♦   ♦   ♦

Seminoles and blacks saw a lot of action for close to twenty years. According to the records, they took part in twenty battles, captured over 430 horses and mules, and killed at least thirty-eight of the enemy without losing a single one of their own men. A Mexican general spoke of them as "always triumphant." Maybe he exaggerated. But there is little doubt that the black and red Seminoles did a good job as border guards. At the same time, they were busy farming in order to support their families.

Horse was rarely out of danger. One year Texas desperadoes kidnapped him and held him for a five-hundred-dollar ransom. (That would equal several thousand dollars today.) Wild Cat paid in gold, staining the coins with blood to remind the kidnappers that they were criminals—dealing in blood money. Horse also survived assassination attempts.

As refugees and foreigners, the Seminoles were careful in dealing with the Mexican people. Various Mexican leaders tried to involve the Americans in the Mexicans' quarrels with one another. Horse refused. Rosa Fay, a woman who had lived in the colony, remembered that he said, "Here we are all living as in one house. How can I take up a gun and kill you, who are my brother, or how can I take up a gun for you and kill that other man, who is also my brother?" It was the same in everyday relationships, Fay recalled. "John Horse would never even let the little children fight with the Mexican children, because he said, 'When we came, fleeing slavery, Mexico was a land of freedom and the Mexicans spread out their arms to us.' "

♦   ♦   ♦

The Mexican community of red and black Seminoles began to break up in the late 1850s. Wild Cat died in 1857. Most Seminoles then returned to Indian Territory in the United States. In the 1860s came the Civil War and, finally, an end to slavery. It now seemed safer for the black Seminoles to return to what was, after all, their native land.

What's more, the United States *wanted* the black Seminoles to return. In 1870 the army sent a captain to Mexico with an offer: If black Seminole men would join the U.S. Army as scouts, the American government would pay their way to Texas and give them and their families food and land.

About fifty black Seminoles accepted the offer. They

formed a special unit known as the Seminole Negro-Indian Scouts. Over the next decade they proved themselves to be superb trackers. Traveling swiftly and with few rations, they could pick up a week-old trail and find the outlaws, rustlers, or Indian raiders who had left it. One of their commanding officers described them as "excellent hunters and trailers, and brave scouts."

The black Seminole nation of about three hundred or more settled down at Forts Duncan and Clark in Texas. They became the first nation of African ancestry to enter the United States as a people.

Horse was too old to serve as a scout himself. What he tried to do was gain justice for his people. Months and then years went by, but the army failed to make good on its promise of land for the scouts' families. Instead, the wives, children, and parents of the scouts had to settle temporarily outside various army posts. Horse tried in vain to get the U.S. government to live up to its word. On file in Washington, D.C., is a petition (signed with an *X*) in which he speaks of his people as his children. "I want to see all my children have their right," he said, "as I brought them all here." Nothing worked.

Finally Horse gave up and returned to Mexico. He served again as a leader of the community of black Seminoles. (Some had remained from the original settlement, and others had joined later.) Horse never stopped working for the benefit of his people. His last known service was a trip to Mexico City in 1882, when it looked as if black Seminoles in Mexico might lose their lands. Horse received a guarantee that this would not happen. Tired and ill, he entered a Mexico City hospital, where—as "Juan Caballo"—he died on August 9. As for the black Seminole scouts, they were gradually retired from service. And their

The Seminole Negro Indian Scouts, photographed in 1889, may have been the toughest desert fighters the U.S. Army had.

families had to leave the army posts where they had settled.

John Horse's life ended in disappointment. But his years of struggle were not forgotten. As late as the 1940s black Seminoles preserved personal memories of this dedicated and resourceful leader. They proudly spoke of him as the "father of his people." They still do.

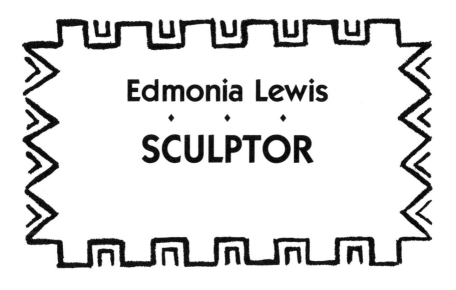

Edmonia Lewis
• • •
SCULPTOR

Winter brought cold and snow to the little town of Oberlin, Ohio. It was a time for sleigh rides and hot drinks around roaring fires. The year was 1862. The Civil War, which had begun a few months earlier, was not going well for the North. But the people of Oberlin had other things on their minds. They were thinking about poison, and a mystery.

The mystery involved students at Oberlin College. Though the college was small, it was known all over the United States. It had been one of the first in the country to admit women. It was also one of the few colleges to welcome African-American students. At the time of this story there were about thirty black students at the college. One of them, of black and Indian ancestry, was Edmonia Lewis. Along with several young white students, she boarded at the home of a local minister. Two of her closest friends there were Maria Miles and Christina Ennes.

One Monday morning late in January, Maria and Christina were getting ready to go on a sleigh ride with two young men. Their journey would take them to Christina's home, several hours away. Wouldn't they like a hot drink of wine before they left? asked Edmonia. Certainly, the two agreed. In her room Edmonia heated wine and added some spices. She drank only a sip, but the two travelers finished theirs before running down the steps and jumping into the waiting sleigh.

A few miles from Christina's home both young women became violently ill. Their friends whipped on the horses so that the sleigh could reach the Ennes home quickly. The family put Maria and Christina to bed and called the doctor.

Rumors flew. The young women had been poisoned and might die. The wine was at fault. And the person responsible for it was Edmonia Lewis.

Strangely, no action was taken. Even the local newspaper printed nothing about the event. As the days went by it became clear that Maria and Christina would live. But it seemed equally clear that something had gone very wrong. The situation was too much for some Oberlin townspeople, who could not understand why Edmonia was still free. One evening early in February, when Edmonia was out walking, one or more people grabbed her, carried her to a field, and beat her badly.

Finally the authorities stepped in. They arrested Edmonia. And they set February 26 as the date for a hearing. Now both town and college hoped to solve the mystery.

♦   ♦   ♦

Who was Edmonia Lewis? When she became well known later in life, several writers interviewed her. This is what she told one of them:

Edmonia Lewis, or Wildfire, who became the first important African-American sculptor, was proud of her African and Indian ancestry.

My mother was a wild Indian and was born in Albany, of copper color and with straight black hair. There she made and sold moccasins. My father, who was a Negro and a gentleman's servant, saw her and married her. . . . Mother often left home and wandered with her people, whose habits she could not forget, and thus we, her children, were brought up in the same wild manner. Until I was twelve years old, I led this wandering life, fishing and swimming . . . and making moccasins.

A few more details might be added. Edmonia's mother was a Chippewa. Her father was a freed slave. The year of her birth was 1845, and the place somewhere near Albany, New York. Edmonia's Indian name was Wildfire, and she had a brother named Sunrise. She once told another interviewer that she lived among the Chippewas to fulfill a promise to her mother. "When my mother was dying," Edmonia said, "she wanted me to promise that I would live three years with her people, and I did." Thus Edmonia's mother must have died when the young girl was only nine.

In 1860, when she was sixteen, Edmonia entered Oberlin, where she was supported by her brother. He sent her money from California, where he had done well during the gold rush that began in 1849. Her father must have died, because she was described at Oberlin as an orphan.

Edmonia's college expenses may have been paid in part by abolitionists. These were reformers who wanted to abolish—that is, get rid of—slavery. Abolition groups first came into being in the early 1800s. They soon spread throughout the northern states. Both blacks and whites belonged. They tried to persuade Congress to outlaw slavery. They urged slave owners to free their slaves. They also helped slaves escape and aided free people of color, like Edmonia.

Oberlin College was a center of abolition activity. The

cause inspired hundreds of students and their teachers, too. The town itself was the home of many free African Americans, and most other townspeople also opposed slavery. Both college and town may have tried to keep the poisoning scandal a secret to protect a black student. And they may have wanted to protect the abolition movement as well. Abolitionists had many opponents, who used any excuse to attack them. But by February 1862 silence was no longer possible.

◆　　　◆　　　◆

Edmonia Lewis was lucky. She had a good lawyer, John Mercer Langston. Himself a graduate of Oberlin, he was probably the only African American practicing law in Ohio in 1862. His father was a white Virginia plantation owner. Interestingly, his mother, like Edmonia, was a mixture of black and Indian.

Langston prepared carefully. He studied the medical aspects of the case and conducted several interviews. At the hearing many witnesses spoke for the prosecution and against Edmonia Lewis. They included Maria and Christina (now recovered), the two young men who had accompanied them, and three doctors. Edmonia never testified. Langston had no witnesses for the defense. But by cross-examination he destroyed the prosecution's case. He showed that no evidence remained from the young women's illness. Therefore, there was simply no proof of poisoning. The court agreed that Edmonia could not be proved guilty and released her.

Langston's autobiography, published many years later, called the Lewis affair "a rare and interesting case." Langston, though a smart man, was not a modest one. He described his argument as "from first to last commanding the closest attention, and at times moving all who heard it to tears." When his client was freed, he wrote, she "was carried in the arms of her excited associates and fellow-students from the court room."

Langston went on to become dean of the law school at Howard University, a diplomat, and a U.S. congressman from Virginia. (He was also a great-uncle of the writer Langston Hughes.) His client, Edmonia Lewis, went on to become the first well-known American woman of color to be a sculptor.

◆　　◆　　◆

"I had always wanted to make the forms of things." This is how Edmonia Lewis in 1864 explained her ambition to the writer Lydia Maria Child. She spoke proudly of her Chippewa mother and her African-American father and of her three years as a child living and working with the Chippewas. She also told Mrs. Child: "Some praise me because I am a colored girl, and I don't want that kind of praise. I would rather you would point out my defects, for that will teach me something." Lewis had moved to Boston right after the trial, without graduating from Oberlin. With her she had a letter introducing her to the best-known abolitionist of the time, William Lloyd Garrison.

Lewis told Garrison about her interest in "making forms"—that is, sculpture. So he sent her to a Boston sculptor named Edmund Brackett. Brackett gave Lewis some clay and the model of a human foot. "Go home and make that," he said. "If there is anything in you, it will come out." Lewis's first attempt was so clumsy that Brackett smashed it. But he suggested that she try again. This time her work showed promise. Brackett encouraged his pupil to continue.

Lewis promptly rented a studio and set to work. She produced her first two important sculptures in 1864. One was a medallion (a sort of large medal) showing the head of John Brown. A famous abolitionist, Brown had been executed five years earlier after leading a raid to free slaves. The second Lewis sculpture was a bust of Colonel Robert Gould Shaw. This white officer from Boston commanded a famous black regiment, the Fifty-fourth Massachusetts, in the Civil War. He and many of his men were killed at the battle of Fort Wagner, in South Carolina, in 1863.

Lewis, who had seen Shaw only once, based her sculpture on photographs. After visiting Lewis's studio with a friend, Lydia Maria Child wrote:

> I confess when she first mentioned her intention of making a bust of Col. Shaw from photographs, I feared she would make a lamentable failure. But when I went to see the bust in clay, I was very agreeably surprised. . . . I thought the likeness extremely good. . . . We both felt that there was something inexpressibly beautiful and touching in the efforts of a long oppressed race to sanctify the memory of their martyr. . . . As we went out into the street, she said to me, "If I were a Spiritualist, I should think Col. Shaw came to aid me about that bust; for I thought, and thought, and thought how he must have looked when he led them to Fort Wagner; and at last it seemed to me as if he was actually in the room."

Lewis exhibited her bust of Shaw to the public, and people liked it so much that she sold a hundred copies of it. The money she earned made it possible for her to go

to Italy in 1865. As far as we know, she lived in Rome—
except for a few trips to the United States—for the rest
of her life.

◆　　　◆　　　◆

In Edmonia Lewis's day Europe attracted artists the way
Hollywood attracts actors today. This had been true since
colonial times. Living was cheap. Museums were filled
with masterpieces. The countryside was beautiful. And
wealthy families liked to buy works of art to decorate their
homes. Italy appealed especially to sculptors because of
its deposits of fine marble.

Europe undoubtedly had additional appeal for Edmonia Lewis as a woman, and a woman of color. Rome
was already the home of several woman sculptors. They
helped and encouraged one another. And they felt free
to lead independent lives, without the pressure of family
responsibilities.

As for Lewis's Indian and African heritage, it was not
the handicap it would have been in the United States.
Many Americans of color, especially artists and writers,
have seen Europe as an escape from prejudice and discrimination in their own country. In Lewis's time the best-
known American black painter, Henry Ossawa Tanner,
settled in Europe as a young man. So, more recently, did
such famous African-American writers as Richard Wright
and James Baldwin.

◆　　　◆　　　◆

Lewis made a name for herself in Rome. She followed the
common practice of modeling works in clay and then hav-

ing them carved in marble by craftsmen. Tourists and the wealthy visited her studio to admire and buy. She also shipped sculptures back to the United States for exhibit and sale. A newspaper article of 1871 described her as follows:

> Edmonia Lewis is below the medium height, her complexion and features betray her African origin; her hair is more of the Indian type, black, straight, and abundant. She wears a red cap in her studio, which is very picturesque and effective; her face is a bright, intelligent and expressive one. Her manners are child-like, simple, and most winning and pleasing.

Like many Europeans and Americans of the time, Lewis followed the style called neoclassical, meaning a modern version of ancient Greek and Roman art. This style valued order and beauty more than emotion and realism. A famous neoclassical statue of George Washington shows him wearing a toga, like a Roman statesman.

Some of Lewis's sculptures are based on myths or religion. One is a cupid. Another shows a Madonna and child. But her best-known works fall into two main groups. One grew out of her African-American background, the other out of her Indian heritage.

The overwhelming black experience of Lewis's own lifetime was the emancipation of slaves after the Civil War. It is the subject of *Forever Free*. This marble sculpture shows a young black man standing proudly. A broken chain dangles from his wrist. At his side kneels a young woman, her hands clasped in prayer. Lewis also sculpted a bust of President Lincoln, who signed the Emancipation Proclamation. In addition, she did busts of prominent abolitionists, such as Wendell Phillips.

Some of Lewis's Native American subjects were inspired by poetry. Two of these are *The Wooing of Hiawatha* and *The Marriage of Hiawatha*. A visitor described them in these words:

> [The former] represents Minnehaha seated making a pair of moccasins, and Hiawatha by her side with a world of love and longing in his eyes. In the marriage [sculpture] they stand side by side with clasped hands. In both, the Indian type of features is carefully preserved, and every detail of dress is true to nature.

Lewis also did a bust of the author of *The Song of Hiawatha*, Henry Wadsworth Longfellow. A different Native American subject is the *Old Indian Arrowmaker and His Daughter*. Both the craftsman and the young girl, dressed in skins, gaze alertly outward as if interrupted by the viewer.

Edmonia Lewis's most famous work was *The Death of Cleopatra*. It was exhibited in Philadelphia in 1876, at the fair honoring the hundredth anniversary of American independence. Twelve feet high and weighing two tons, the sculpture was called by one viewer "the grandest statue in the exposition." Apparently, Lewis showed the dying Egyptian queen in a very realistic way. A fellow sculptor wrote that the piece "was not a beautiful work, but it was a very original one." He went on to say that "the effects of death are represented with such skill as to be absolutely repellent."

Lewis had a reputation for blunt realism. She talked honestly about her hard life as a Chippewa and at Oberlin.

Forever Free, Edmonia Lewis's sculpture celebrating the emancipation of the slaves after the Civil War. Courtesy of the Howard University Gallery of Art

Some visitors found in her face the "sadness of African and Indian races."

◆　　◆　　◆

Little is known of Edmonia Lewis's life after 1876. President Grant posed for her in the winter of 1877–1878. The year after that she was in the United States to present a bust of John Brown to a black abolitionist. At some time she became a Roman Catholic. The pope visited her studio once and blessed a sculpture she was modeling. In the 1880s the famous African-American leader Frederick Douglass reported seeing her "oddly dressed" figure in Rome. A directory published in 1911 listed her residence as Rome. After that, there is silence.

The neoclassical style went out of fashion in the late 1800s. Did Lewis continue to work in it? Did she continue to work at all? Was she poor? Was she alone? Probably no one will ever know. In keeping with her Chippewa name, Wildfire, she blazed briefly and then disappeared. But whatever happened to her, she had been a pioneer.

George Henry White
MILITANT CONGRESSMAN

"Mr. Chairman," said the man from North Carolina, "I am here to speak, and I do speak, as the sole representative on this floor of nine million of the population of these United States." Standing his full six feet two, he continued: "We want something now upon which soul and body can be kept together. We want an honest dollar. We want pay for an honest day's work."

The man was George Henry White. The occasion was his first speech in Congress, on March 31, 1897. The goal White wanted—honest pay for honest work—was shared by most Americans. But the new congressman did indeed speak for one large group. These were the nation's African Americans. At this time White was the only black man in Congress. He was unusual in other ways, too. He was the last former slave to serve in the national legislature. And after his two terms in office, no black person would serve in Congress for almost thirty years.

White spoke on several topics during his four years in

Congress. But in almost every speech he sooner or later brought up the subject of African Americans, and the injustices they suffered. His outspokenness made him unpopular among many whites, both in his home state and in Congress. Some African Americans also worried that his speeches would only antagonize whites. But he would not be silenced, for he believed in his cause with all his heart.

◆   ◆   ◆

George White was born in southeastern North Carolina in 1852. His ancestors included Native Americans, African Americans, and Irish Americans. But White identified fully with his black ancestors. His father was a slave, and so was he.

Practically nothing is known of White's youth. He learned the basics at local public schools. He may have gotten a late start. He was thirteen when the Civil War ended, freeing the slaves. Only then were black children able to attend public school. White continued his education at Howard University, paying his way by teaching school during the summer. He graduated in 1877 with a teaching certificate. He then studied with a lawyer in New Bern, North Carolina. Two years later he became a lawyer himself. He also got married.

◆   ◆   ◆

The year of White's graduation from Howard marked the end of Reconstruction. This twelve-year period began after the Civil War. The word "reconstruction" means rebuilding. This was the task the United States faced in 1865. It

Congressman George Henry White fought alone for people of color in the U.S. Congress between 1897 and 1901.

had to repair the damage caused by the war. Even more important, it had to deal with human problems, especially those concerning the four million former slaves. They were poor, and few of them could read or write.

Americans did not handle the human problems of Reconstruction very well. White southerners were full of mistrust and bitterness. Some resented losing the war and their slaves. Abraham Lincoln had been assassinated at the end of the war. The new president, Andrew Johnson, lacked Lincoln's human understanding and good sense. He was prejudiced against people of color. Politicians split along party lines. Congress was in the hands of Republicans, while most white southerners were Democrats.

Almost all the ex-slaves went to work as farmers. They could not afford to buy their own land, so they worked for others in return for miserable wages. Some worked for the same families that had owned them as slaves. Others struck out on their own. The federal government set up schools to teach them reading and writing and adopted new laws and constitutional amendments to protect their civil rights. Former slaves could now vote, hold office, and serve on juries. Few white southerners wanted to share power, however. They formed secret organizations, including the Ku Klux Klan, that used violence and terror to try to keep people of color "in their place."

To see that the laws were obeyed, the federal government stationed troops in the southern states. With their protection freed slaves voted, and they elected black men to their state legislatures and to Congress. Between 1869 and 1901, twenty African Americans served in the House of Representatives and two served in the Senate. All of them were Republicans. Blacks felt great loyalty to the Republican party because Republicans—Lincoln above all—had controlled the northern government that won the war.

Keeping troops in the South cost money. As time went on, more and more white northerners resented this expense. White southerners, of course, had opposed it from the beginning. Racism played a big part, too. Most white

Americans, in the North as well as in the South, regarded black people as inferior. Few cared whether they had equal rights with whites. White southerners wanted to be left alone to handle the "Negro problem" in their own way. White northerners decided to let them do so.

Reconstruction ended in 1877, when the government withdrew the last federal troops from the South. The next few years were a time of uneasy race relations in the region. White Democrats controlled most southern states. They tried to keep African Americans from voting. But in many areas blacks continued to vote.

◆　　◆　　◆

George White was an ambitious man with a good education. He soon became interested in Republican politics. In the 1880s he moved to Tarboro, in eastern North Carolina, where many black people lived. In several counties there African Americans outnumbered whites, and so could elect black officials. They elected George White to the state House of Representatives and, later, to the state Senate. There he worked to improve public schools, especially for African-American children.

In 1885 White was elected prosecutor for the district in which he lived. This meant that he had to supervise criminal cases brought against people who broke the law. According to one newspaper account, he was a "terror to evildoers" in court.

In 1896 White ran for the U.S. Congress and won. Election returns showed that he had received many white as well as black votes. The same thing was happening elsewhere in the South, too. In other words, reform-minded white (Democratic) and black (Republican) voters

53

were working together. Both groups were angry at the conservative Democrats in power. Times were hard. Farmers found that their crops were earning less money every year. They accused politicians in power of ignoring their needs. In the 1890s more than half the workers in the country were farmers. They were much more important as a political force than they are today. Together, African Americans and reform-minded whites were able to elect many black Republicans—like White—and reform Democrats to office.

◆   ◆   ◆

White entered Congress in March 1897. At this time the chief spokesman for African Americans in the United States was Booker T. Washington, born just four years after George Henry White. Head of Tuskegee Institute in Alabama, Washington had a strong personality and a wonderful speaking style. His message to his people was this: Work hard, learn a trade, and don't offend whites by making a lot of political demands. In a famous speech of 1895, he said:

> To those of my race who depend upon bettering their condition in a foreign land or who underestimate the importance of cultivating friendly relations with the Southern white man . . . I would say "Cast down your bucket where you are"—cast it down in making friends in every manly way of the people of all races by whom we are surrounded. Cast it down in agriculture, in mechanics [industry], in commerce, in domestic service, and in the professions.

Booker T. Washington, seated third from the left, at Tuskegee Institute, which he founded and where he served for many years as president. On the right of Washington is inventor and millionaire Andrew Carnegie, who contributed to Tuskegee.

White did not oppose Washington in public, as far as we know. But he could not follow the educator's advice to keep quiet about racial injustice. White hinted at his feelings in a letter to Booker T. Washington in 1902, after he left Congress. He disagreed, he said, with Washington's position that took him "in an entirely different direction from that of politics." At the same time, though, he admired Washington's "noble achievements . . . in behalf of our people. I always take off my hat," wrote White, "to the man who has *accomplished something*."

In Congress, White wasted no time in speaking up for the "nine million of the population" he represented. His very first speech dealt mainly with trade. But he also made it clear that referring to blacks as "darkies"—which many southern Democrats did—was wrong and unacceptable.

White was always a loyal Republican. For instance, he supported the Republican administration in the Spanish-American War of 1898. He also approved of adding new territories, such as the Philippines and Puerto Rico, after the war. But he continued to stand up for African Americans, too. He reminded Congress that "charity begins at home." He spoke out against the brutal murder of a black South Carolina postmaster and his infant son. He criticized Mississippi for tampering with black voting returns. He also delivered a warning and a prophecy about the "Negro problem":

> You will have to meet it. You have got this problem to settle, and the sooner it is settled the better it will be for all parties concerned. I speak this in all charity. I speak this with no hostility. I am not a pessimist. I take rather the other view. I am optimistic in my views and believe that these problems will adjust themselves one day. I believe that the Negro problem in less than fifty years will be a thing of the past.

White ran for reelection to Congress in 1898. By this time an ugly trend was becoming obvious in the South. Democratic politicians did not like being opposed by an alliance of white reformist Democrats and black Republicans. So they used racism to split the opposition and win back the white vote. They frightened whites who voted with or for African Americans, accusing them of bringing about "Negro domination." And they frightened blacks who voted at all, threatening them with loss of jobs and with violence.

In North Carolina an organization called the Red Shirts

held parades and warned people against being "ne-groized." Just before the November election a Democratic politician appealed to voters to "restore the state to the white people."

North Carolina is a WHITE MAN'S STATE, and WHITE MEN will rule it, and they will crush the party of negro domination beneath a majority so overwhelming that no other party will ever again dare to establish negro rule here.

This campaign was successful. North Carolina voters returned conservative Democrats to power in the state. Many African Americans were simply too frightened to vote. But not all. In spite of threats, enough of them turned out to reelect George White. Two days later, however, a white riot in Wilmington resulted in the deaths of ten black citizens. The local newspaper boasted that "Negro rule is at an end in North Carolina forever."

The same thing was going on elsewhere in the South. Throughout the region, conservative white Democrats had returned to power in the late 1890s. Now they didn't rely only on threats of violence to keep African Americans from voting. They went further and disfranchised them—that is, they took away their right to vote. States did this in many ways. For instance, they might require a very high poll tax—a fee charged every voter. Or they might set up polling booths in places blacks could not reach. North Carolina passed a law disfranchising most African Americans in 1900.

This was not all. Southern states passed new restrictions requiring strict segregation of the races. Earlier, they had set up separate school systems for black and white children. Beginning in the 1890s, so-called Jim Crow regulations went much further. African Americans had to use separate railroad cars, streetcars, restaurants, and public toilets and water fountains. In theaters, they had to sit in the balcony. In some courtrooms, they even had to swear on a separate Bible!

◆　　　◆　　　◆

George White's second term in the House of Representatives began in 1899. He knew that it would be his last, and probably the last for any African American for years to come. But he continued to speak out courageously on behalf of African Americans.

The single most important thing White did in Congress was to introduce a bill in January 1901. It had the very ordinary title of HR [House of Representatives] 6963. But it was a milestone—the first attempt to get Congress to outlaw lynching.

Lynching is mob action that kills, often by hanging. For years it was common in the South, though it occurred in the North as well. Sometimes lynch mobs broke into jails and seized people accused of crimes before they went on trial. At other times lynch mobs attacked citizens in their homes or at work. Between 1884 and 1900, lynchings averaged almost 150 a year. The vast majority of the victims were black males in the South.

White had attacked lynching during his first term. "If a man commits a crime . . . he ought to be punished," said White. "But he ought to be punished according to the law as administered in a court of justice."

In a speech to Congress made soon after introducing his bill, White listed some of the "crimes" of which black

A black man is asked to leave his seat in a segregated railroad car.

men had been accused. Along with murder, barn burning, and assault were these: "talked too much"; "brother to murderer"; "wanted to work"; and "spoke against lynching."

Our constitutional rights have been trodden under foot; our right of franchise in most every one of the original slave States has been virtually taken away from us, and during the time of our freedom fully 50,000 of my race has been ignominiously murdered by mobs, not 2 percent of whom have been made to answer for their crimes in the courts of justice.

White's bill did not pass. It had at least two strikes against it. One was the racist feeling of the times. The other was the severe penalty for breaking the law. White's bill provided that anyone taking part in a lynching had to be convicted of treason (and thus subject to the death penalty).

As White came to the end of his years in Congress, he must have felt disappointed that the bill did not pass. But his very last speech, given on January 29, 1901, was an eloquent defense of African Americans:

You may tie us and then taunt us for a lack of bravery, but one day we will break the bonds. You may use our labor for two and a half centuries and then taunt us for our poverty, but let me remind you we will not always remain poor. You may withhold even the knowledge of how to read God's word and learn the way from earth to glory and then taunt us for our ignorance, but we would remind you that there is plenty of room at the top, and we are climbing.

He ended on a note of determination:

This, Mr. Chairman, is perhaps the Negroes' temporary farewell to the American Congress, but let me say . . . he will rise up some day and come again. These parting words are in behalf of an outraged, heartbroken, bruised, and bleeding but God-fearing people, faithful, industrious, loyal people—rising people, full of potential force.

When White left Congress, he is said to have remarked: "I cannot live in North Carolina and be a man." True to his word, he never lived in the state again. He stayed on in Washington, D.C., for a few years, where he practiced law. Later he moved to Philadelphia.

Although he was no longer a politician, White continued to promote African-American interests. He founded the first black-managed bank in Philadelphia, the People's Savings Bank. He also bought two thousand acres of land near Cape May, New Jersey. There he founded the town of Whitesboro as a place where African Americans could live in peace and safety. The town had a population of several hundred at the time of White's death in 1918.

White did not live to see African Americans regain their vote, nor the end of Jim Crow. But he could be proud of his part in keeping alive the struggle for equality. As one historian put it: "He had the thankless task of defending the rights of his people during a period of maximum oppression in which the national conscience rested in a deep slumber."

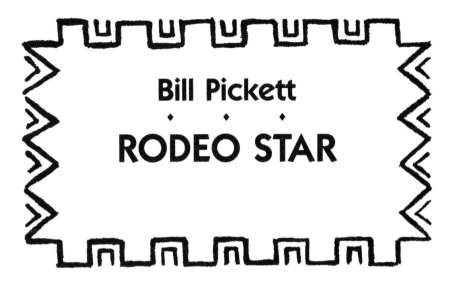

Bill Pickett
• • •
RODEO STAR

He wears jeans, a ten-gallon hat, and boots. He's more at home on a horse than in a car. His speech is somewhere between a drawl and a twang. He is the westerner, an American hero. Books, movies, and television shows have made him familiar all over the world. Sometimes he makes a living as a rancher or a law enforcer. Usually, though, he's a cowboy.

When we think of cowboys we think of tall white men like John Wayne. But real cowboys have always come in all sizes and colors. The very first cowboys, in fact, were Mexicans, often a mixture of Spanish and Indian peoples. Black cowboys have been common, too. In the late 1800s and early 1900s few were better known than Bill Pickett.

Pickett was born near Austin, Texas, in 1870. His father, a former slave, was of mixed African-American, white, and Cherokee background. His mother has been described as a blend of "black, Mexican, white, and Indian."

The Pickett family made a living by farming. But as soon as the children (there were thirteen) could go to work, they did so. Bill finished fifth grade and was then pretty much on his own. Like many youngsters in Texas at the time, he was drawn to the life of cattle ranches and cowboys. He would be part of it for the rest of his life.

♦　　♦　　♦

Cattle had roamed the plains of Texas for centuries. The best known were Texas longhorns. This tough breed had horns that sometimes stretched five feet across. Longhorns might wander many miles looking for grass. There were no fences to pen them in. (Thus the land was known as open range.) Each rancher could identify his own cattle because they were marked with his brand.

In the early days, ranchers sold their cattle locally for meat and hides. But a bigger market opened up after the Civil War. This happened because railroad companies began building their lines across the West. Cattle could then be shipped by train to the East. That was where the big cities were—big cities full of people who liked to eat beef.

The first western railroads did not go through Texas. They crossed Missouri, Kansas, and Colorado, farther north. So cattle had to be driven north to the rail lines. Cowboys, mounted on horseback, rounded up cattle on the open range. Then they drove thousands of them to towns like Abilene and Dodge City. The "long drive," as it was called, was hard, dangerous work. But the men who took part in it captured the imagination of the public. They were regarded as rugged individualists who got the job done. People, especially Americans, liked to think of these qualities as typically American.

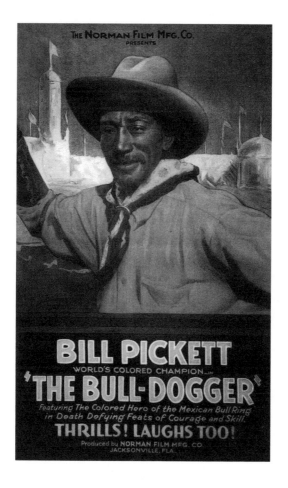

This silent-movie poster announces Bill Pickett's skill as a "bull-dogger."

♦   ♦   ♦

A cowboy had to ride well. He had to be able to rope a calf or a steer that was running loose. This meant whirling a lariat, dropping it around the animal's neck or horns, and pulling the creature to a stop. Some cowhands had to be broncobusters—able to cling to the back of an un-tamed horse so that it could be trained to be ridden.

Another cowboy skill, bulldogging, involved grabbing an animal's horns and twisting its neck so that it fell to the ground. Cowhands used bulldogging when brush and trees made roping difficult. It also came in handy at brand-ing time, when cattle had to be held down to be branded. The odd name came from the time ranchers trained dogs to grab an animal's upper lip and hang on. The pain and the bulldog's weight made the animal stay put until a cowboy could rope it.

Bill Pickett was fascinated by bulldogging. He had the idea of combining the human and animal ways of doing it. One day he tried with no one watching. He walked up to a calf and seized its ears. Then he dug his teeth into its upper lip and wrestled the surprised animal to the ground.

Soon afterward young Bill told some cowboys about what he could do. He may have bragged a little, but who could blame him? The cowboys laughed. But Bill showed them that he was telling the truth. Word spread. After that, young Pickett could work as a cowboy just about anywhere in the Austin area.

♦   ♦   ♦

The ranchers and cowboys of Bill Pickett's time were set-tling the last frontier—the West of the Great Plains and Rocky Mountains. They were part of the same movement that had drawn Americans westward ever since the 1600s. A lot of other people were also moving into this region. Miners moved east after the California gold rush, search-ing everywhere for precious metals. Railroad workers, many of them Irish or Chinese, came to lay the tracks that would link the Pacific Coast with the rest of the country. Farmers came, too. Even though much western land was dry and treeless, it could grow bumper crops of wheat. Each of these groups included blacks. Many former slaves were eager to make a fresh start in a new part of the country.

All these people were newcomers. Long before they appeared, the region had been the home of Native Americans. Most of them (like the Crows among whom Edward Rose lived) lived as buffalo hunters. They had been promised millions of acres by the government. But whites wanted the land. And, as in the East, they got it. Over the years the Indians were forced to turn over their territory and settle on reservations. Some, like the Sioux leaders Crazy Horse and Sitting Bull, fought to stay on their hunting grounds. But sooner or later, army troops forced all the Indians to give up. The last holdout was Geronimo of the Apaches, who surrendered in 1886.

People of the late 1800s loved reading about cowboys and Indians. To take advantage of this interest, William Cody, known as Buffalo Bill, a rancher and former buffalo hunter, organized what he called the Wild West show. The first one took place in 1883 at North Platte, Nebraska. Wild West shows were very popular from this time until about 1920.

A Wild West show was a spectacle, like the circus. An opening parade would feature bands and all the performers, riding on horseback. There were always several dramatic episodes. One might show a stagecoach robbery. Another might feature a buffalo hunt or a battle between Indians and army cavalry. (Sitting Bull toured with Buffalo Bill's show for one season.)

A Wild West show also had contests of skill. In this way it was like a rodeo, another form of entertainment that was developing at the same time. Cowboys roped calves and rode broncos. They also staged displays of fancy riding, rope tricks, and marksmanship.

Women—"cowgirls"—took part in Wild West shows, too. They excelled at trick riding. And one of the most famous of all Wild West performers was Annie Oakley, a great sharpshooter. She could hit dimes tossed in the air and drill six holes in a playing card before it fell to the ground.

Both Wild West shows and rodeos had plenty of cowboys to choose from after the late 1800s. The era of the open range had come to an end. When ranchers fenced in their herds, long drives were no longer necessary. So, many cowboys were out of a job.

♦   ♦   ♦

Bill Pickett began to display his bulldogging skills at rodeos when he was still in his teens. He could make a little money by winning prizes. Besides, he liked to perform. He got married in 1890. With children (eventually nine) to support, the money looked even better.

By the early 1900s Pickett was performing all over the West. Rodeos, like Wild West shows, were attracting national attention. The best known included the Cheyenne Frontier Days in Wyoming and the Calgary Stampede in Alberta, Canada. Billed as "the Dusky Demon," Pickett appeared at both of these exhibitions and many others as well. Here is how a Denver newspaper described his act in 1904:

To pick out the best feature of yesterday afternoon's events is quite impossible, for every number on the program was good. But if there is special mention to be made William Pickett, the Texas Negro cowboy, who twice threw unaided a wild steer with his teeth, is deserving it. . . . [Pickett] loped down the home stretch mounted on a horse and caught up with the steer that had been turned loose a little in advance of his start. . . . The silence of expectation which settled over the grandstand as the horse drew near the lumbering brute, deepened to a dead calm as the Negro's horse dashed alongside the animal, catching the stride of the steer, and then the Negro leaped from his horse to the steer's back. Pickett wound himself around the animal's neck and fastened his teeth in its upper lip.

Then, with a series of quick jerky movements the Negro forced the steer to its knees and rolled it over on its side. . . . He again jumped on the back of the steer, which in the meantime regained its feet, and repeated the performance.

In Pickett's own words: "I reach over the top of his head with my teeth—what's left of 'em—and throw myself back mighty hard, and the steer he kirflollops on the ground—sometimes he lights on me—sometimes he doesn't."

◆   ◆   ◆

One of the most famous Wild West shows was the 101 Ranch Wild West Show. It was started in 1905 by the Miller family of Oklahoma. They named it after their huge 101 Ranch, near Ponca City. Pickett joined the show in 1907. Like many of the performers, he worked on the Miller ranch when the show was not on the road.

Pickett was one of the stars of the Millers's show. His main act, of course, was bulldogging. Because of him, this cowboy trick became a regular part of Indian and rodeo shows. Few other cowboys followed Pickett's example of "taking a mouthful," however. And as time went on, he himself stopped doing so. (Today the event is called steer wrestling, or "Bill Pickett bulldogging.")

Pickett performed other unusual feats, too. One time he wrestled a bull elk to the ground. He had a bad experience once in Mexico City. The Millers advertised that Pickett would grapple with a Mexican fighting bull for at least five minutes. This was very hard because such a bull is much bigger than the standard rodeo steer. Pickett managed to hang on to the bull's horns for over five minutes. But his only reward from the huge crowd was boos. Expecting something like the classic bullfight, they regarded Pickett's performance as an insult.

Pickett might be a star. But in everyday life he and his family had to live in a Jim Crow world. His children attended a segregated school. It was set up in a church for the Picketts and the other five African-American families in their Oklahoma town. One of Pickett's closest friends was a white druggist. If the two men wanted to have dinner together, the druggist had to go to a restaurant and order takeout. Then he and Pickett would eat it at the drugstore. No black people were allowed to eat in the restaurant.

◆　　　◆　　　◆

The 101 Ranch Wild West Show toured throughout the United States in the early 1900s. With all its performers, horses, cattle, wagons, and special equipment, it required twenty-two railroad cars when moving. The show traveled by ship to South America in 1913 and to England the fol-

This is an announcement for the 101 Ranch Rodeo.

lowing year. At a New York City show in 1916, former president Theodore Roosevelt attended several performances.

But times were changing. A new form of entertainment, the motion picture, was becoming popular. "Westerns" could tell a dramatic story more realistically than a Wild West show could. In fact, many early movie stars began as Wild West performers. Four from the 101 Ranch show were Buck Jones, Hoot Gibson, Will Rogers, and Tom Mix.

The 101 Ranch show began to lose money in the 1920s. Things got worse after 1929, with the beginning of the Great Depression, a terrible business slump. Two years later the Millers's show came to an end.

Pickett had retired from the show in 1917. But he continued to perform from time to time. Sometimes he bulldogged in rodeos, sometimes for the Wild West show. He also continued to work at the Miller ranch. It was here that he met his death in 1932, kicked in the head while trying to rope a bronco. He was buried on the ranch. The owner, Zack Miller, admired Pickett as "the greatest sweat and dirt cowboy that ever lived, bar none." He wrote a poem that began with these lines:

> Old Bill has died and gone away,
> Over the "Great Divide."
> Gone to a place where the preacher says
> Both saint and sinner will abide.
> If they "check his brand" like I think they will
> It's a running hoss they'll give to Bill.
> And some good wild steers till he gets his fill.
> With a great big crowd for him to thrill.

And he ended:

> He left a blank that's hard to fill
> For there'll never be another Bill.
> Both White and Black will mourn the day
> That the "Biggest Boss" took Bill away.

The 101 Ranch Rodeo crew, including Bill Pickett (second row, third from right), Will Rogers (fifth from right), and Tom Mix (seventh from right). Photograph taken in 1914

A HIDDEN HERITAGE

She is a young black woman named Fanny. Every now and then she is overwhelmed by strong feelings for various people long dead. When this happens, her husband, Suwelo, thinks of her as falling in love with spirits.

One day Fanny bursts into their home after discovering a new spirit from the past. He is none other than John Horse, the black Seminole chief. Eyes flashing, she tells her husband what she learned: how Horse fought alongside the Indians, moved west, settled in Mexico, and died there. Suwelo asks her, "What do you love about these people?"—about the "old ones" with whom Fanny seems to fall in love. She replies: "I dunno. They open doors inside me. It's as if they're keys." The inner rooms opened by these "keys," says Fanny, bring her intense happiness.

Fanny and Suwelo are not real people. They are characters in a novel, *The Temple of My Familiar*. Its author, Alice Walker, is an American writer of African and Native American ancestry. She is clearly fascinated by relationships between the two peoples. So are many other Americans who share this heritage.

Many of today's African Americans also have Native American ancestors. In some cases, people don't know very much about the Native Americans in their family tree. If they do know, the facts are few. Here is how Charles Evers, who was elected mayor of Fayette, Mississippi, explains it:

> My Daddy's mother was named Mary, and she was part . . . Indian. She had long, straight hair and high cheekbones. Most black people can go back only to their grandparents. No one kept records. We didn't have birth certificates. Each family had a big old Bible, and usually the momma would put in there when each of the children was born.

Evers did know that he had another Indian ancestor.

> My great-grandfather on my Momma's side was half Indian. He was a slave, but from what I've heard he was one of the worst slaves they'd ever had. He just wouldn't take any abuse.

As you've read, men like Edward Rose and George Henry White had Native American ancestors about whom nothing is known. The same is true of several well-known figures of our own time. Paul Robeson, the great singer and actor, is an example. His mother's ancestors included Delaware Indians. But their names are forgotten. So it is with Jesse Jackson. His great-grandmother was part Cherokee. (Both Robeson and Jackson had white ancestors, too.)

Apache Biddy Johnson Arnold helped raise her grandsons, George and Ed Tooks.

Sometimes a little more information exists. Take the writer Langston Hughes. He knew that one of his great-grandmothers, Lucy Langston, was part Indian. (She was the mother of John Mercer Langston, the lawyer who defended Edmonia Lewis.) And he knew, too, that two other great-grandparents were part Indian. Maybe he thought about them when, in one of his poems, he wrote about "the red man driven from the land."

Another African American with several Indian fore-bears is the singer Lena Horne. One of her great-grand-mothers, Atlanta Fernando, was of French, Hispanic, and Native American descent. Another, according to family legend, was a Blackfoot Indian, married to an Englishman. In her book about the Horne family, Lena's daughter points out that since the Hornes grew up in the South and the Blackfeet lived on the plains, it's more likely that this ancestor was Creek or Cherokee. Anyway, the family tells this story about her:

> She apparently did not lose touch with her spiritual heritage. In summer storms, she made her half-English children stand out in open fields—as electricity danced around their heads—so they would have no fear of nature.

Indian ways have also enriched the lives of two mu-sician brothers, George and Ed Tooks. They were reared in Pennsylvania by their Apache grandmother, Biddy Johnson Arnold. She used to take the two boys to the woods to look for leaves, roots, bark, and berries. These she would turn into medicines for the ailing. Some people traveled many miles for her free concoctions. "You have two different types of blood in your veins," she would tell her grandsons. "Be proud of both."

Probably the best-known explorer of family roots in our time was Alex Haley. His search for his African ances-tors led to his book (and a television series), *Roots*. Haley spent two years and traveled half a million miles to learn the story of Kunta Kinte, his African forebear six gener-

Chief Osceola Townsend (third from left) and Hempstead, Long Island, Mayor James A. Garner (center) at a 1993 ceremony in which the original deed for the sale of the village is returned to the original owners, represented by Chief Osceola of the Matinecock Indians and David Bunn Martine of the Shinnecock Indians (second from left)

ations back. Like many other African Americans who explore their family backgrounds, Haley found a great-grandmother, Irene, who was part Indian.

Thousands of lesser-known Americans are also trying to learn more about their hidden heritage. To aid them, Vivian Ayers-Allen, an African American whose grandfather was Cherokee, established the Adept New American Museum for the Art of the Southwest. Located in Mount Vernon, New York, it stresses the contributions of both African and Native Americans as well as the inter-relationships between the two groups. Education is also one of the aims of Chief Osceola Townsend's Brooklyn-based National Alliance of Native Americans, which attracts people of many ethnic backgrounds to its programs offering both cultural instruction and other assistance.

African-American Zsun-nee Kimball Matema of Silver Spring, Maryland, recently discovered her Native American ancestry, and it changed her life. Her interest in her past was first stirred when she "quite mysteriously and unexpectedly" met Native Americans in southern Maryland. When she attended a slide lecture at the Smithsonian Institution on the book *Black Indians: A Hidden Heritage,* she became fascinated.

She began to research her family history. "My name Matema," she found, "can also be traced from the mountains of Nigeria to the Spanish Sahara in the Sudan, to South Africa, to the Ashanti people of Ghana, to the Aztec Empire in the Americas." A cousin sent her a history book describing the family lineage. From it she learned her Choctaw ancestors lived in Livingston, Alabama, and practiced medicine with herbs and roots.

In 1990 Ms. Matema created a nonprofit theater and women's training company that had two missions. First it was dedicated to help people build bridges across various cultures. Second it tried to aid women of color develop business skills necessary for the twenty-first century.

One of Ms. Matema's theatrical programs, *Poky,* told of the life of Pocahontas Kimball, her Choctaw great-grandmother in Livingston, and "tells why it's important for black Indians to celebrate their dual ancestry."

Ms. Matema has dedicated herself and her theatrical talents to "create works which will help teach the world that we must explore just a little deeper than previously

Zsun-nee Kimball Matema learned she had Choctaw ancestors.

thought before we can judge or classify people by their appearance alone."

Before Alex Haley began his research, he told an elderly relative about his plans. "You go 'head, boy!" exclaimed his cousin Georgia. "Yo sweet grandma an' all of 'em—dey up dere *watchin'* you!" Whether or not we share this feeling, we can feel a sense of wonder as the dim figures of our past are revealed. And we are stronger for knowing something about the chain of beings who brought us to where we are. As Haley put it, "You can never enslave somebody who knows who he is."

BIBLIOGRAPHY

Blodgett, Geoffrey. "John Mercer Langston and the Case of Edmonia Lewis: Oberlin, 1862." *Journal of Negro History* (July 1968).

Buckley, Gail Lumet. *The Hornes.* New York: Knopf, 1986.

Camp, Charles L. "James Clyman, His Discoveries and Reminiscences." *California Historical Quarterly* 4 (1925).

Chittenden, Hiram M. *The American Fur Trade of the Far West.* New York: Press of the Pioneers, 1935.

Christopher, Maurine. *Black Americans in Congress.* New York: Thomas Y. Crowell, 1971.

Civkosky, Nicolai, Jr., Marie H. Morrison, and Carol Ockman. *The White Marmorean Flock.* Poughkeepsie, N.Y.: Vassar College Art Gallery, 1972.

Collings, Ellsworth, and Alma Miller England. *The 101 Ranch.* Norman: University of Oklahoma Press, 1938.

Dale, Harrison. *The Ashley-Smith Explorations.* Cleveland: Arthur H. Clark, 1918.

Evers, Charles. *Evers.* New York: World, 1971.

Felton, Harold W. *Edward Rose: Negro Trail Blazer.* New York: Dodd, Mead, 1967.

Fine, Elsa Honig. *Women and Art: A History of Women Painters and Sculptors from the Renaissance to the 20th Century.* Montclair, N.J.: Allanheld and Schram, 1978.

Foner, Philip S. *History of Black Americans.* Westport, Conn.: Greenwood Press, 1975.

Goetzmann, William. *Exploration and Empire: The Explorer and the Scientist in the Winning of the American West.* New York: Knopf, 1966.

Hallowell, A. Irving. "American Indians, White and Black: The Phenomenon of Transculturalization." *Current Anthropology* 4, no. 5 (December 1963).

Hanes, Bailey C. *Bill Pickett, Bulldogger.* Norman: University of Oklahoma Press, 1977.

Harris, Sheldon H. *Paul Cuffe: Black America and the African Return.* New York: Simon and Schuster, 1972.

Irving, Washington. *The Adventures of Captain Bonneville.* Norman: University of Oklahoma Press, 1961.

———. *Astoria.* Norman: University of Oklahoma Press, 1964.

Katz, William Loren. *Black Indians: A Hidden Heritage.* New York: Atheneum, 1986.

———. "George Henry White: A Militant Negro Congressman in the Age of Booker T. Washington." *Negro History Bulletin* (March 1966).

Lamar, Howard R., ed. *The Reader's Encyclopedia of the American West.* New York: Thomas Y. Crowell, 1977.

Langston, John Mercer. *From the Virginia Plantation to the Nation's Capitol.* Hartford, Conn.: American Publishing, 1894.

Littlefield, Daniel F., Jr. *Africans and Creeks: From the Co-*

lonial Period to the Civil War. Westport, Conn.: Green-wood Press, 1979.

Logan, Rayford. *Dictionary of American Negro Biography.* New York: Norton, 1982.

McLoughlin, William G. "Red Indians, Black Slavery and White Racism: America's Slaveholding Indians." *American Quarterly* 26, no. 4 (October 1974).

Milligan, John D. "Slave Rebelliousness and the Florida Maroon." *Prologue: The Journal of the National Archives* (Spring 1974).

Narrative of the Life and Adventures of Paul Cuffe, a Pequot Indian: During Thirty Years Spent at Sea, and in Travelling in Foreign Lands. Vernon, N.Y.: Horace N. Bill, 1839.

Phillips, Paul C. *The Fur Trade.* Norman: University of Oklahoma Press, 1961.

Porter, James A. *Modern Negro Art.* New York: Dryden Press, 1943.

Porter, Kenneth W. *The Negro on the American Frontier.* New York: Arno Press, 1971.

Ragsdale, Bruce. *Black Americans in Congress, 1870–1989.* Washington: U.S. Government Printing Office, 1990.

Reid, George W. "A Biography of George H. White." Ph.D. dissertation, Howard University, 1974.

Smith, Samuel Denny. *The Negro in Congress, 1870–1901.* Chapel Hill: University of North Carolina Press, 1940.

Thomas, Lamont D. *Rise to Be a People: A Biography of Paul Cuffe.* Urbana: University of Illinois Press, 1986.

Tufts, Eleanor. *Our Hidden Heritage: Five Centuries of Women Artists.* New York: Paddington Press, 1973.

Walker, Alice. *The Temple of My Familiar.* San Diego: Harcourt Brace Jovanovich, 1989.

Woodward, C. Vann. *The Strange Career of Jim Crow.* New York: Oxford University Press, 1966.

INDEX

INDEX